DEATH AND LIFE
ARE IN
THE POWER OF THE TONGUE
(PROVERBS 18:21)

CONFESSION STATEMENTS
BASED ON SCRIPTURE

(A Christian tool to effect Victorious Living)

ALLISON L. JORDAN

ISBN: 1-4033-6607-1 (e-book)
ISBN: 1-4033-6608-X (Paperback)

Library of Congress Control Number: 2002111746

This book is printed on acid free paper.

Printed in the United States of America
Bloomington, IN

1stBooks – rev. 01/29/03

This book is dedicated to my mother Elnora B. Lane for

always encouraging me to be all that God would have

me be

and

to my children, Allison Danielle and Ashta Jovan, whom

I pray will learn to apply these confession statements

to their lives as they grow in the grace and knowledge

of Jesus Christ

ACKNOWLEDGEMENTS

First and foremost, I thank God for loving me so much that he allowed his only begotten son Jesus Christ to die for me while I was yet a sinner. Secondly, I thank Jesus for his obedience. Third, I thank the Holy Spirit for empowering me to write this book and get it into publication.

To my childhood friend, spiritual mentor and sister-in-Christ, Deborah C. Fontaine. Thank you for continuing to love me and pray for me all those years I was a carnal Christian. Thank you for helping me to grow spiritually after I truly decided to follow Jesus and become one of his disciples. You have truly blessed my life and ministry.

To my cousin and spiritual son, Mark A Hardy Jr. who worked alongside me on his book "Vision Through the Eyes of God", while I was working on mine. May God continue to bless you as you continue to live for him.

I thank all of my brothers and sisters in Christ who either supported this project, suggested various scriptures or kept asking me when I was going to publish this work.

A very special thanks to my students in the Bible Institute at Gethsemane Baptist Church, Newport News, Va. for being the catalysts for this project.

My deepest gratitude to my former pastor, Dwight Riddick for helping me to become who I am spiritually and to my current pastor, Raymond L. Lassiter, Jr. for letting me be who I have become.

Thank you to Joyce Meyer, T.D. Jakes, Andy Wommack, Juanita Bynum and all the other televangelists and preachers/teachers who have played a major part in my spiritual growth (unbeknownst to them).

Thanks to my neighbor and sister-in Christ, Lula Horton, for double-checking the accuracy of my scripture references.

Finally, I thank 1st Books for helping to make this dream come true.

PREFACE

LUKE 4:4

MAN SHALL NOT LIVE BY BREAD ALONE BUT BY EVERY **WORD OF GOD** (KJV)

HEBREWS 4:12

FOR THE **WORD OF GOD** IS FULL OF LIVING POWER. IT IS SHARPER THAN THE SHARPEST KNIFE, CUTTING DEEP INTO OUR INNERMOST THOUGHTS AND DESIRES. IT EXPOSES US FOR WHAT WE REALLY ARE. (NEW LIVING)

PROVERBS 30:5

EVERY **WORD OF GOD** IS PURE; HE IS A SHIELD UNTO THEM THAT PUT THEIR TRUST IN HIM (KJV)

ISAIAH 40:8

THE GRASS WITHERS AND THE FLOWERS FALL, BUT THE **WORD OF GOD** STANDS FOREVER (NIV)

PROVERBS 18:4

A PERSON'S **WORDS** CAN BE LIFE-GIVING WATER; **WORDS** OF TRUE WISDOM ARE AS REFRESHING AS A BUBBLING BROOK (NEW LIVING)

ISAIAH 55:11

SO SHALL **MY WORD** BE THAT GOETH FORTH OUT OF MY MOUTH; IT SHALL NOT RETURN UNTO ME VOID, BUT IT SHALL ACCOMPLISH THAT WHICH I PLEASE, AND IT SHALL PROSPER IN THE THING WHERETO I SENT IT (KJV)

INTRODUCTION

IN THE GOSPELS OF MATTHEW (4:1-11) AND LUKE (4:1-13), JESUS GIVES CHRISTIANS THE MODEL FOR DEALING WITH TEMPTATIONS (ATTACKS) FROM SATAN. IN EACH OF THE THREE INSTANCES WHERE SATAN ATTEMPTED TO PREVENT JESUS FROM FULFILLING HIS MISSION, JESUS RESPONDED IN THE SAME WAY. HE DID NOT ENGAGE IN DISCUSSION OR ARGUMENT WITH THE DEVIL. HE RESPONDED BY STATING "**IT IS WRITTEN**" (KJV/NIV) FOLLOWED BY **GOD'S WORD** ON THE SUBJECT.

IN SHORT, HE **SPOKE** THREE CONFESSION STATEMENTS TO SATAN. IMMEDIATELY AFTERWARDS, THE GOSPEL OF MATTHEW 4:11 RECORDS THAT "**THE DEVIL LEFT HIM, AND ANGELS CAME AND ATTENDED HIM**". THE GOSPEL OF LUKE 4:13 RECORDS THAT "**WHEN THE DEVIL HAD FINISHED ALL THIS TEMPTING, HE LEFT HIM UNTIL AN OPPORTUNE TIME**". (NIV)

AMAZINGLY, MANY CHRISTIANS TODAY DO NOT UTILIZE THIS SIMPLE PRINCIPLE (EITHER DUE TO LACK OF KNOWLEDGE OR BECAUSE THEY HAVE UNDERESTIMATED THE IMMEASURABLE VALUE OF THIS BIBLICAL TOOL). AS A RESULT, THEY ARE OVERWHELMED AND SUBSEQUENTLY DEFEATED BY THOUGHTS, EMOTIONS AND EVENTS THAT THE ENEMY BRINGS INTO THEIR MINDS AND LIVES.

ALTHOUGH, I TOO, STRUGGLE WITH CERTAIN ISSUES, IT IS MY BELIEF AND PERSONAL TESTIMONY THAT OUR LEVEL OF FAITH CAN BE DIRECTLY CORRELATED TO OUR BELIEF IN GOD AND THE **APPLICATION OF HIS WORD** IN OUR DAILY LIVES. THEREFORE, WHENEVER SATAN ATTACKS OUR THOUGHTS OR ORCHESTRATES EVENTS IN OUR LIVES THAT ARE CONTRARY TO THE WILL OF GOD, WE MUST **SPEAK THE WORD OF GOD TO HIM AND TO OURSELVES.** FOLLOWING JESUS' EXAMPLE TO DO SO (BASED ON FAITH IN GOD AND IN CONJUNCTION WITH REGULAR PRAYING AND SPIRIT-LED FASTING) WILL DEVELOP OUR FAITH AND RESULT IN MORE FRUITFUL AND VICTORIOUS WALKS WITH GOD.

CONTENTS

WHEN YOU ARE:

WHEN YOU ARE GOING THROUGH AND SATAN INVITES YOU TO A "PITY PARTY"

CONFESS...

JESUS SAID THAT IN THIS LIFE I WILL HAVE TRIBULATION BUT THAT I SHOULD BE OF GOOD CHEER BECAUSE HE HAS OVERCOME THE WORLD (ST. JOHN 16:33)

MANY ARE THE AFFLICTIONS OF THE RIGHTEOUS BUT GOD WILL DELIVER ME FROM THEM ALL (PSALMS 34:19)

I WILL STAND STILL AND SEE THE SALVATION OF THE LORD (EX 14:13) FOR MY GOD IS ABLE TO DELIVER ME (DAN 3:17)

THE LORD IS MY ROCK, AND MY FORTRESS, AND MY DELIVERER; MY GOD, MY STRENGTH, IN WHOM I WILL TRUST; MY BUCKLER AND THE HORN OF MY SALVATION, AND MY HIGH TOWER (PS 18:2 KJV)

THE ANGEL OF THE LORD ENCAMPETH ROUND ABOUT THEM THAT FEAR HIM AND DELIVERETH THEM; OH TASTE AND SEE THAT THE LORD IS GOOD; BLESSED IS THE MAN THAT TRUSTETH IN HIM (PSALM 34:7-8 KJV)

MY SUFFERINGS OF THIS PRESENT TIME ARE NOT WORTHY TO BE COMPARED WITH THE GLORY WHICH SHALL BE REVEALED IN ME (ROM 8:18)

GOD IS MY REFUGE AND STRENGTH, AN EVER-PRESENT HELP IN TROUBLE (PS 46:1)

I WILL REJOICE IN MY SUFFERINGS BECAUSE SUFFERING PRODUCES PERSEVERANCE; PERSEVERANCE, CHARACTER; AND CHARACTER, HOPE (ROMANS 5:3-4)

BLESSED IS THE MAN/WOMAN WHO PERSEVERES UNDER TRIAL BECAUSE WHEN HE/SHE HAS STOOD THE TEST, HE/SHE WILL RECEIVE THE CROWN OF LIFE THAT GOD HAS PROMISED (JAMES 1:12)

MY SOUL WAITETH UPON GOD; FROM HIM COMETH MY SALVATION. HE ALONE IS MY ROCK AND MY SALVATION; HE IS MY DEFENSE; I SHALL NOT BE GREATLY MOVED (PS 62:1-2 KJV)

_____

_____

_____

_____

_____

_____

_____

Allison L. Jordan

_____

_____

_____

_____

_____

_____

_____

_____

_____

_____

WHEN SATAN TELLS YOU GOD DID NOT HEAR

OR WILL NOT ANSWER YOUR PRAYERS

CONFESS...

THIS IS THE CONFIDENCE I HAVE IN HIM; THAT IF I ASK ANYTHING ACCORDING TO HIS WILL, HE HEARS ME AND SINCE I KNOW HE HEARS ME, I KNOW THAT I WILL HAVE THE PETITIONS I ASKED OF HIM (I JOHN 5:14-15)

WHATEVER I ASK THE FATHER IN THE NAME OF JESUS WILL BE GIVEN TO ME (ST. JOHN 16:23)

I ABIDE IN JESUS AND HIS WORDS ABIDE IN ME, SO I CAN ASK WHAT I WILL AND IT SHALL BE DONE (ST. JOHN 15:7)

WHEN I PRAY, I BELIEVE THAT I HAVE RECEIVED WHAT I ASKED FOR (MATTHEW 21:22)

AS A CHILD OF GOD, I CAN PRAY FOR ANYTHING AND IF I BELIEVE, I CAN HAVE IT (MARK 11:24)

I DELIGHT MYSELF IN THE LORD, SO HE WILL GRANT ME THE DESIRES OF MY HEART (PSALMS 37:4)

WHAT GOD HAS PROMISED ME, HE IS ABLE TO PERFORM (RO 4:21)

I KNOW HE HEARD AND WILL ANSWER MY PRAYER, FOR GOD IS NOT A MAN THAT HE SHOULD LIE (NUM 23:19)

PRAISE BE TO GOD WHO HAS NOT REJECTED MY PRAYER OR WITHHELD HIS LOVE FROM ME (PS 66:20)

THE SPIRIT OF GOD IN ME GUARANTEES HE WILL GIVE ME EVERYTHING HE PROMISED (EPH 1:14)

_____

_____

_____

_____

_____

_____

_____

_____

_____

_____

_____

_____

_____

_____

_____

Allison L. Jordan

_____

_____

_____

_____

_____

_____

_____

_____

_____

_____

<u>WHEN YOU ARE AFRAID</u>

CONFESS...

THE LORD IS MY LIGHT AND MY SALVATION; WHOM SHALL I FEAR? HE PROTECTS ME FROM DANGER, I WILL NOT TREMBLE (PS 27:1)

GOD HAS NOT GIVEN ME A SPIRIT OF FEAR, BUT OF POWER, LOVE AND A SOUND MIND (II TIM 1:7)

EVEN THOUGH I WALK THROUGH THE VALLEY OF THE SHADOW OF DEATH, I WILL FEAR NO EVIL FOR THE LORD IS WITH ME; HIS ROD AND STAFF PROTECT AND COMFORT ME (PS 23:4)

I WILL NOT BE AFRAID OF THE TERRORS BY NIGHT OR THE DANGERS OF THE DAY, FOR THE LORD ORDERS HIS ANGELS TO PROTECT ME WHEREVER I GO (PS 91:5,11)

I WILL NOT BE AFRAID OF SUDDEN DISASTER OR TROUBLE FROM THE WICKED WHEN IT COMES, FOR THE LORD IS MY CONFIDENCE (PROV 3:25)

I WILL NOT BE AFRAID BECAUSE GOD IS WITH ME (ISAIAH 41:10)

I WILL WALK IN GOD'S PERFECT LOVE WHICH CASTS OUT FEAR (I JOHN 4:18)

I WILL NOT BE AFRAID OF WHAT MAN CAN DO TO ME, IN GOD HAVE I PUT MY TRUST (PS 56:11)

GOD IS MY SALVATION; I WILL TRUST AND NOT BE AFRAID FOR THE LORD JEHOVAH IS MY STRENGTH AND MY SONG (ISA 12:2 KJV)

I WILL NOT BE AFRAID OF EVIL TIDINGS; MY HEART IS FIXED AND I TRUST IN THE LORD (PS 112:7)

_____

_____

_____

_____

_____

_____

_____

_____

_____

_____

_____

_____

_____

_____

_____

Allison L. Jordan

WHEN YOU ARE DISCOURAGED OR DEPRESSED

CONFESS...

I WILL NOT BE DEJECTED OR SAD, THE JOY OF THE LORD IS MY STRENGTH (NEH 8:10)

WHY AM I DISCOURAGED? WHY AM I SAD? I WILL PUT MY HOPE IN GOD, I WILL PRAISE HIM AGAIN, MY SAVIOR AND MY GOD (PS 42:5 NLT)

I WILL FORGET MY COMPLAINT, I WILL LEAVE OFF MY HEAVINESS AND COMFORT MYSELF (JOB 9:27 KJV)

I WILL ENCOURAGE MYSELF IN THE LORD (I SAM 30:6)

I WILL PUT ON A GARMENT OF PRAISE FOR MY SPIRIT OF HEAVINESS (ISAIAH 61:3)

I WILL GIVE THANKS TO THE FATHER WHO HAS QUALIFIED ME TO SHARE IN THE INHERITANCE IN THE KINGDOM OF LIGHT. I WILL REJOICE IN THE FACT THAT I HAVE BEEN RESCUED FROM THE DOMINION OF DARKNESS AND BROUGHT INTO THE KINGDOM OF THE SON HE LOVES IN WHOM I HAVE REDEMPTION AND THE FORGIVENESS OF SINS (COL 1:12-14)

THE JOY OF JESUS REMAINS IN ME SO THAT MY JOY CAN BE FULL (ST.JOHN 15:11)

THIS IS THE DAY THE LORD HAS MADE; I WILL REJOICE AND BE GLAD IN IT (PS 118:24)

I WILL NOT BE DISCOURAGED FOR THE LORD GOES BEFORE ME. HE WILL BE WITH ME, HE WILL NOT FAIL OR FORSAKE ME (DEUT 31:8)

I WILL BE STRONG AND COURAGEOUS. I WILL NOT BE AFRAID OR DISCOURAGED. FOR THE LORD MY GOD IS WITH ME WHEREVER I GO (JOSH 1:9)

_____

_____

_____

_____

_____

_____

_____

_____

_____

_____

Allison L. Jordan

_____

_____

_____

_____

_____

_____

_____

_____

_____

_____

WHEN YOU ARE WORRIED/ANXIOUS

CONFESS...

I CAST ALL MY CARES ON JESUS; FOR HE CARES ABOUT ME (I PETER 5:7)

I WILL BE CAREFUL FOR NOTHING; BUT IN EVERYTHING BY PRAYER AND SUPPLICATION WITH THANKSGIVING I WILL MAKE MY REQUESTS KNOWN TO GOD (PHIL 4:6)

I WILL NOT WORRY ABOUT TOMORROW, TOMORROW WILL WORRY ABOUT ITSELF (MATT 6:34)

WORRY WEIGHS ME DOWN; AN ENCOURAGING WORD WILL CHEER ME UP (PROV 12:25)

I WILL NOT LET MY HEART BE TROUBLED; JESUS HAS GIVEN ME HIS PEACE (ST. JOHN 14:27)

I CAST MY CARES ON THE LORD SO HE WILL SUSTAIN ME; HE NEVER LETS THE RIGHTEOUS FALL (PS 56:22)

I WILL NOT LET THE CARES OF THIS WORLD CAUSE THE WORD IN ME TO BECOME UNFRUITFUL (MARK 4:19)

WORRY WILL NOT ADD A SINGLE HOUR TO MY LIFE (LUKE 12:25)

I HAVE FAVOUR AND GOOD UNDERSTANDING IN THE SIGHT OF GOD AND MAN (PROV 3:4)

THE LORD COMFORTS ME WHEN I AM TROUBLED SO THAT I CAN COMFORT OTHERS (II COR 1:4)

_____

_____

_____

_____

_____

_____

_____

_____

_____

_____

_____

_____

_____

Allison L. Jordan

_____

_____

_____

_____

_____

_____

_____

_____

_____

_____

_____

WHEN STRUGGLING WITH ADDICTIONS OR UNGODLY HABITS (EVEN WHEN YOU ARE SAVED)

CONFESS...

I MUST REMEMBER THAT HE THAT IS IN THE FLESH CANNOT PLEASE GOD (ROM 8:8)

I MUST PUT ON THE LORD JESUS CHRIST SO THAT I WILL NOT MAKE PROVISION FOR THE FLESH TO FULFILL THE LUSTS THEREOF (ROM 13:14)

I WILL NOT BE IN BONDAGE TO THIS HABIT FOR I AM MORE THAN A CONQUEROR THROUGH CHRIST WHO LOVES ME (ROM 8:37)

I WILL NOT SPEND THE REST OF MY DAYS CHASING AFTER EVIL DESIRES OF THE FLESH; INSTEAD I WILL BE ANXIOUS TO DO THE WILL OF GOD AND HAVE THE SAME MIND AS CHRIST JESUS. HE SUFFERED FOR ME SO I WILL SUFFER FOR HIM AND STOP SINNING (I PETER 4:1-2)

I WILL PUT ON THE WHOLE ARMOUR OF GOD (THE BELT OF TRUTH, HELMET OF SALVATION, BREASTPLATE OF RIGHTEOUSNESS, SHOES OF PEACE, SHIELD OF FAITH, HIS WORD AND PRAYER) SO I CAN STAND AGAINST THE STRATEGIES AND TRICKS OF THE DEVIL (EPH 6:11-18)

I MUST BELIEVE THAT I CAN DO ALL THINGS THROUGH CHRIST WHO STRENGTHENS ME (PHIL 4:13)

I WILL NOT DECEIVE MYSELF; MY GOD WILL NOT BE MOCKED. IF I CONTINUE TO SOW TO THE FLESH, I WILL REAP A CORRUPTED HARVEST FULL OF DECAY AND DEATH (GAL 6: 7-8)

I WILL CLEANSE MYSELF FROM ALL FILTHINESS OF THE FLESH AND SPIRIT BY THE POWER OF THE HOLY SPIRIT WITHIN ME (II COR 7:1)

I CONFESS THAT I HAVE BEEN CRUCIFIED WITH CHRIST. THEREFORE IT IS NO LONGER I THAT LIVE BUT CHRIST JESUS WHO LIVES IN ME (GAL 2:20)

I WILL WALK IN THE SPIRIT AND NOT FULFILL THE LUST OF THE FLESH FOR THE FLESH LUSTS AGAINST THE SPIRIT AND THE SPIRIT AGAINST THE FLESH (GAL 5:16-17)

_____

_____

_____

_____

_____

_____

Allison L. Jordan

_____

_____

_____

_____

_____

_____

_____

_____

_____

_____

_____

<u>WHEN YOU ARE PERSECUTED (LIED ON OR TALKED ABOUT) FOR RIGHTEOUSNESS' SAKE</u> CONFESS...

NO WEAPON THAT IS FORMED AGAINST ME SHALL PROSPER AND EVERY TONGUE THAT RISES UP AGAINST ME SHALL BE CONDEMNED SAITH THE LORD (ISAIAH 54:17)

SINCE THEY PERSECUTED JESUS, NATURALLY THEY WILL PERSECUTE ME. A SERVANT IS NOT GREATER THAN HIS MASTER (ST.JOHN 15:20)

I WILL NOT CURSE THOSE WHO PERSECUTE ME BECAUSE I AM A CHRISTIAN, I WILL PRAY THAT GOD WILL BLESS THEM (ROM 12:14)

GOD WILL PROTECT ME FROM WICKED PEOPLE WHO ATTACK ME; HE WILL GUARD ME AS THE "APPLE OF HIS EYE" AND HIDE ME IN THE SHADOW OF HIS WINGS (PS 17:8-9)

BLESSED ARE THEY WHO ARE PERSECUTED BECAUSE THEY ARE RIGHTEOUS; THEIRS IS THE KINGDOM OF HEAVEN (MATT 5:10)

I WILL FRET NOT BECAUSE OF EVILDOERS NOR BE ENVIOUS OF THOSE WHO DO WRONG, FOR LIKE GRASS THEY WILL SOON FADE AWAY AND LIKE FLOWERS THEY WILL SOON WITHER (PS 37:1)

I MUST SHARE IN CHRIST'S SUFFERINGS SO THAT I MAY SHARE IN HIS GLORY (ROM 8:17)

I WILL NOT AVENGE MY ENEMIES FOR IT IS WRITTEN; "VENGEANCE IS MINE," SAYS THE LORD (ROM 12:19)

IN HIS JUSTICE, GOD WILL PUNISH THOSE WHO PERSECUTE ME (II THES 1:6) AND HE WILL TURN INTO GOOD WHAT WAS MEANT FOR EVIL AGAINST ME (GEN 50:20)

EVEN IN THE PRESENCE OF MINE ENEMIES, GOD PREPARES A TABLE BEFORE ME. HE ANOINTS MY HEAD WITH OIL, MY CUP OVERFLOWS. SURELY GOODNESS AND MERCY SHALL FOLLOW ME ALL THE DAYS OF MY LIFE, AND I WILL DWELL IN THE HOUSE OF THE LORD FOREVER. (PS 23:5-6 NIV)

_____

_____

_____

_____

_____

_____

_____

_____

_____

_____

Allison L. Jordan

_____

_____

_____

_____

_____

_____

_____

_____

_____

WHEN YOUR FINANCES ARE UNDER ATTACK OR YOU HAVE FINANCIAL NEED

CONFESS...

THE LORD IS MY SHEPHERD; I SHALL NOT WANT (PS 23:1 KJV)

I SEEK GOD FIRST AND HIS RIGHTEOUSNESS, EVERYTHING I NEED WILL BE ADDED TO ME (MATT 6:33)

THE LORD IS MY PROVIDER; HE WILL PROVIDE BECAUSE HE IS JEHOVAH JIREH (GEN 22:14)

MY GOD WILL SUPPLY ALL MY NEEDS ACCORDING TO HIS RICHES IN GLORY BY CHRIST JESUS (PHIL 4:19)

I GO BOLDLY BEFORE THE THRONE OF GRACE TO OBTAIN MERCY AND FIND GRACE TO HELP ME IN MY TIME OF NEED (HEB 4:16)

I HAVE LACK OF NOTHING BECAUSE I WALK HONESTLY TOWARD THEM THAT ARE WITHOUT (I THES 4:12)

MY FATHER KNOWS MY NEED EVEN BEFORE I ASK HIM (MATT 6:8)

I HAVE NEVER SEEN THE RIGHTEOUS FORSAKEN OR THEIR SEED BEGGING BREAD (PS 37:25)

JESUS PROMISED ME ABUNDANT LIFE (ST. JOHN 10:10) AND GOD IS NOT A MAN THAT HE SHOULD LIE (NUM 23:19 KJV)

MY WAY IS MADE PROSPEROUS AND I WILL HAVE GOOD SUCCESS BECAUSE I MEDITATE ON GOD'S WORD DAY AND NIGHT AND I DO WHAT HE INSTRUCTS ME TO DO (JOSH 1:8)

_____

_____

_____

_____

_____

_____

_____

_____

_____

_____

_____

_____

_____

_____

_____

_____

Allison L. Jordan

_____

_____

_____

_____

_____

_____

_____

_____

_____

_____

_____

<u>WHEN YOU ARE LONELY AND FEEL LIKE NOBODY</u>

<u>CARES ABOUT YOU</u>

CONFESS...

OH WHAT A FRIEND I HAVE IN JESUS, A FRIEND THAT STICKS CLOSER THAN A BROTHER. I HAVE NO GREATER LOVE THAN THE FACT THAT (WHILE I WAS YET A SINNER) JESUS LAID DOWN HIS LIFE FOR ME AND HE CONSIDERS ME HIS FRIEND (PROV 18:24, ST.JOHN 15:13,15)

GOD HAS PROMISED ME THAT HE WILL NEVER LEAVE ME OR FORSAKE ME (HEB 13:5)

I AM COMPLETE IN JESUS WHO IS THE HEAD OF ALL PRINCIPALITIES AND POWER (COL 2:10)

THE LORD HAS PROMISED ME THAT HE WILL ALWAYS BE WITH ME UNTIL THE END OF THE EARTH (MATT 28:20)

I WILL GREATLY REJOICE IN THE LORD, MY SOUL SHALL BE JOYFUL IN MY GOD; FOR HE HATH CLOTHED ME WITH THE GARMENTS OF SALVATION, HE HATH COVERED ME WITH THE ROBE OF RIGHTEOUSNESS, AS A BRIDEGROOM DECKETH HIMSELF WITH ORNAMENTS, AND AS A BRIDE ADORNETH HERSELF WITH HER JEWELS. (ISAIAH 61:10 KJV)

I AM PERSUADED THAT NOTHING CAN SEPARATE ME FROM THE LOVE OF GOD WHICH IS IN CHRIST JESUS (ROM 8:39)

THE LORD DOES NOT FORSAKE THOSE THAT SEEK HIM (PS 9:10)

BECAUSE OF THE LORD'S GREAT LOVE, I AM NOT CONSUMED, FOR HIS COMPASSIONS NEVER FAIL; THEY ARE NEW EVERY MORNING; GREAT IS HIS FAITHFULNESS (LAM 3:22-23)

THE PRESENCE OF GOD IS WITH ME AND HE GIVES ME REST (EX 33:14)

JESUS CARES FOR ME, I WILL CAST MY LONELINESS UPON HIM (I PET 5:7)

_____

_____

_____

_____

_____

_____

_____

_____

_____

_____

Allison L. Jordan

_____

_____

_____

_____

_____

_____

_____

_____

_____

<u>WHEN GOD SAYS "NO" OR THINGS DON'T GO</u>

<u>ACCORDING TO YOUR PLANS</u>

CONFESS...

GOD KNOWS THE PLANS HE HAS FOR ME, PLANS TO PROSPER ME AND NOT TO HARM ME, PLANS TO GIVE ME HOPE AND A FUTURE (JER 29:11)

NOT MY WILL LORD, BUT YOUR WILL BE DONE (MARK 14:36) BECAUSE WHATEVER IS GOOD AND PERFECT WILL COME TO ME FROM GOD ABOVE (JAMES 1:17)

I WILL REMEMBER THAT NO DISCIPLINE SEEMS PLEASANT AT THE TIME; IN FACT IT IS PAINFUL, BUT EVENTUALLY IT WILL PRODUCE A HARVEST OF RIGHTEOUSNESS AND PEACE FOR THOSE WHO HAVE BEEN TRAINED BY IT (HEB 12:11)

EYE HAVE NOT SEEN, NOR EAR HEARD, NEITHER HAVE ENTERED INTO THE HEART OF MAN THE THINGS WHICH GOD HATH PREPARED FOR ME BECAUSE I LOVE HIM (I COR 2:9)

OH WHAT A WONDERFUL GOD I HAVE! HOW GREAT ARE HIS RICHES AND WISDOM AND KNOWLEDGE! HOW IMPOSSIBLE IT IS FOR ME TO UNDERSTAND HIS DECISIONS AND HIS METHODS! FOR WHO CAN KNOW WHAT THE LORD IS THINKING? WHO KNOWS ENOUGH TO BE HIS COUNSELOR? TO HIM BE THE GLORY FOREVER (ROM 11:33-36)

WHAT I WANTED MUST NOT BE BEST FOR ME FOR NO GOOD THING WILL GOD WITHHOLD FROM ME BECAUSE I WALK UPRIGHTLY (PS 84:11)

ALL THINGS WILL WORK TOGETHER FOR MY GOOD BECAUSE I LOVE THE LORD AND AM CALLED ACCORDING TO HIS PURPOSE (ROM 8:28)

I MADE PLANS, BUT THE LORD DETERMINED MY STEPS (PROV 16:9)

GLORY BE TO GOD! BY HIS MIGHTY POWER AT WORK WITHIN ME, HE IS ABLE TO DO INFINITELY MORE THAN I COULD EVER DARE TO ASK, HOPE OR THINK (EPH 3:20)

GOD'S WAYS ARE NOT MY WAYS, HIS THOUGHTS ARE NOT MY THOUGHTS (ISAIAH 55:8)

_____

_____

_____

_____

_____

_____

_____

Allison L. Jordan

_____

_____

_____

_____

_____

_____

_____

_____

_____

_____

<u>WHEN YOU ARE SICK IN YOUR BODY AND CAN'T</u>

<u>SEEM TO GET WELL</u>

CONFESS...

BY JESUS' STRIPES (WOUNDS) I AM HEALED; HE BORE MY SINS ON A TREE SO THAT I WOULD DIE TO SIN AND LIVE FOR RIGHTEOUSNESS (I PET 2:24)

MY PRAYER OFFERED IN FAITH WILL HEAL ME AND THE LORD WILL MAKE ME WELL (JAMES 5:16)

JESUS CAN HEAL ALL MANNER OF SICKNESS AND DISEASE (MATT 4:23) SPEAK A WORD LORD, AND I WILL BE HEALED (MATT 8:8)

THE LORD IS MY HEALER (EX 15:26)

THE LORD WILL SUSTAIN ME ON MY SICKBED AND RESTORE ME FROM MY BED OF ILLNESS (PS 41:3)

I LIVE BY GOD'S WORDS FOR THEY ARE LIFE TO THOSE THAT FIND THEM AND HEALTH TO MY FLESH (PROV 4:22)

I WILL CRY OUT TO GOD AND HE WILL HEAL ME (PS 30:2)

BECAUSE I FEAR THE LORD, THE SUN OF RIGHTEOUSNESS WILL RISE WITH HEALING IN HIS WINGS (MAL 4:2)

THE LORD WILL RESTORE HEALTH UNTO ME AND HEAL ME OF MY WOUNDS (JER 30:17)

THE LORD WILL TAKE THIS SICKNESS FROM ME BECAUSE I WORSHIP HIM (EX 23:25)

_____

_____

_____

_____

_____

_____

_____

_____

_____

_____

_____

_____

_____

_____

_____

_____

_____

_____

_____

_____

_____

_____

_____

_____

_____

_____

WHEN YOU ARE HAVING A CRISIS OF FAITH

CONFESS...

WITHOUT FAITH IT IS IMPOSSIBLE TO PLEASE GOD, FOR HE THAT COMES TO GOD MUST BELIEVE THAT HE IS AND THAT HE IS A REWARDER OF THOSE WHO DILIGENTLY SEEK HIM (HEB 11:6)

LORD, FORGIVE MY UNBELIEF, FOR THERE IS NOTHING TOO HARD FOR YOU (JER 32:17)

THE GOSPEL OF CHRIST ASSURES ME THAT GOD HAS MADE ME RIGHTEOUS IN HIS SIGHT FROM START TO FINISH AND IT IS WRITTEN THAT THE JUST (RIGHTEOUS) SHALL LIVE BY FAITH (ROM 1:17)

I HAVE FAITH IN GOD SO I WILL SAY TO MY MOUNTAIN (WITHOUT DOUBT BUT BELIEF THAT THE THINGS I SAY SHALL COME TO PASS) "BE REMOVED AND CAST INTO THE SEA" (MARK 11:22-23)

THE TESTING OF MY FAITH DEVELOPS PERSEVERANCE WHICH MUST FINISH ITS PERFECT WORK SO I WILL BE MATURE AND COMPLETE (JAMES 1:3-4)

FAITH COMETH BY HEARING AND HEARING THE WORD OF GOD (ROM 10:17)

I AM A RIGHTEOUS PERSON; I WILL LIVE BY FAITH, FOR GOD HAS NO

PLEASURE IN ANYONE WHO TURNS AWAY (HEB 10:38)

I WILL FIGHT THE GOOD FIGHT OF FAITH AND LAY HOLD ON ETERNAL

LIFE (I TIM 6:12)

I WILL WALK BY FAITH AND NOT BY SIGHT (II COR 5:7)

_____

_____

_____

_____

_____

_____

_____

_____

_____

_____

_____

_____

_____

_____

Allison L. Jordan

_____

_____

_____

_____

_____

_____

_____

_____

_____

_____

_____

WHEN SATAN WHO IS THE "ACCUSER OF THE

BRETHREN" TRIES TO CONVINCE YOU THAT

YOU ARE NOT *REALLY* SAVED OR BORN

AGAIN BECAUSE OF YOUR PAST

CONFESS...

I AM SAVED BY GRACE THROUGH FAITH AND NOT OF MYSELF; IT IS THE GIFT OF GOD (EPH 2:8)

WHO WILL BRING ANY CHARGE AGAINST ME WHOM GOD HAS CHOSEN? IT IS GOD WHO JUSTIFIES (ROM 8:33)

I DID NOT CHOOSE JESUS; HE CHOSE ME AND NO MAN CAN PLUCK ME OUT OF JESUS' OR GOD'S HAND (ST. JOHN 15:16, 10:28-29)

GOD MADE JESUS *WHO KNEW NO SIN* TO BE SIN FOR ME SO THAT I MIGHT BE MADE THE RIGHTEOUSNESS OF GOD IN HIM (II COR 5:21)

I AM NOW LED BY THE SPIRIT, I AM A CHILD OF GOD, I HAVE RECEIVED THE SPIRIT OF ADOPTION WHEREBY I CRY ABBA, FATHER. THE SPIRIT OF GOD TESTIFIES WITH MY SPIRIT THAT I AM GOD'S CHILD SO I AM AN HEIR OF GOD AND A CO-HEIR WITH JESUS (ROM 8:14-17)

GOD HAS BEGUN A GOOD WORK IN ME AND HE WILL CONTINUE UNTIL THE DAY OF JESUS DEVELOPING, PERFECTING AND BRINGING IT TO COMPLETION IN ME (PHIL 1:6)

THE BLOOD OF JESUS CHRIST HAS CLEANSED ME FROM ALL SIN BECAUSE I WALK IN THE LIGHT AS HE IS IN THE LIGHT (I JOHN 1:7)

ALL HAVE SINNED AND FALLEN SHORT OF THE GLORY OF GOD BUT I AM JUSTIFIED BY THE GRACE OF GOD THROUGH THE REDEMPTION OF JESUS CHRIST (ROM 3:23-24)

THE LORD WILL PRESENT ME FAULTLESS BEFORE THE PRESENCE OF HIS GLORY WITH EXCEEDING JOY (JUDE 1:24)

I HAVE BEEN SEALED BY THE HOLY SPIRIT OF GOD UNTIL THE DAY OF REDEMPTION (EPH 4:30)

_____

_____

_____

_____

_____

_____

_____

_____

_____

Allison L. Jordan

_____

_____

_____

_____

_____

_____

_____

_____

_____

_____

_____

WHEN TEMPTED BY SATAN TO GO BACK TO SOMETHING OR SOMEONE YOU HAVE BEEN DELIVERED FROM

CONFESS...

I AM A NEW CREATURE IN CHRIST; OLD THINGS HAVE PASSED AWAY AND ALL THINGS HAVE BECOME NEW (II COR 5:17)

I HAVE SUBMITTED MYSELF UNTO GOD; I AM RESISTING YOU DEVIL AND I COMMAND YOU TO FLEE FROM ME (JAMES 4:7)

I HAVE PUT OFF THE OLD MAN WITH HIS DEEDS AND HAVE PUT ON THE NEW MAN WHICH IS RENEWED IN KNOWLEDGE AFTER THE IMAGE OF HIM THAT CREATED HIM (COL 3:9-10)

I AM FORGETTING THE THINGS THAT ARE BEHIND ME AND LOOKING FORWARD TO THE THINGS THAT LIE AHEAD; I AM PRESSING TOWARD THE MARK FOR THE PRIZE OF THE HIGH CALLING OF GOD IN CHRIST JESUS (PHIL 3:13-14)

I DO NOT REMEMBER THE FORMER THINGS NOR DO I CONSIDER THE THINGS OF OLD. GOD IS DOING A NEW THING IN ME (ISAIAH 43:18-19)

WHEN SINNERS ENTICE ME; I WILL NOT CONSENT (PROV 1:10)

I AM DEAD IN THAT AREA AND MY LIFE IS HIDDEN WITH CHRIST IN GOD (COL 3:3)

THIS TEMPTATION IS NO DIFFERENT THAN OTHERS HAVE EXPERIENCED. AND GOD IS FAITHFUL, HE WILL KEEP THIS TEMPTATION FROM BECOMING SO STRONG THAT I CAN'T STAND UP AGAINST IT. AS I AM BEING TEMPTED, HE WILL SHOW ME A WAY OUT SO I WILL NOT GIVE IN TO IT (I COR 10:13)

I WILL AVOID IT, PASS NOT BY IT, TURN FROM IT AND PASS AWAY (PROV 4:15)

I WILL NOT BE UNEQUALLY YOKED WITH UNBELIEVERS; FOR THERE IS NO FELLOWSHIP BETWEEN RIGHTEOUSNESS AND UNRIGHTEOUSNESS AND NO COMMUNION BETWEEN LIGHT AND DARKNESS (II COR 6:14)

_____

_____

_____

_____

_____

_____

_____

_____

_____

Allison L. Jordan

_____

_____

_____

_____

_____

_____

_____

_____

_____

_____

_____

<u>WHEN SATAN SAYS YOU CAN NEVER BE</u>

<u>PERFECT OR LIVE HOLY</u>

CONFESS...

I AM PERFECT JUST AS MY FATHER WHO IS IN HEAVEN IS PERFECT (MATT 5:48)

I AM A TEMPLE OF GOD AND THE HOLY SPIRIT LIVES WITHIN ME (I CORIN 3:16) THEREFORE GOD ENABLES ME TO SERVE HIM WITHOUT FEAR IN HOLINESS AND RIGHTEOUSNESS BEFORE HIM ALL OF MY DAYS (LUKE 1:74-75)

GOD HAS MADE ME PERFECT IN EVERY GOOD WORK TO DO HIS WILL; HE IS WORKING IN ME THAT WHICH IS PLEASING TO HIS SIGHT (HEB 13:21)

I FOLLOW HOLINESS AND PEACE WITH ALL MEN SO I CAN SEE THE LORD (HEB 12:14)

THE DIVINE POWER OF GOD HAS GIVEN ME EVERYTHING I NEED FOR LIFE AND GODLINESS THROUGH MY KNOWLEDGE OF HIM WHO HAS CALLED ME BY HIS OWN GLORY AND GOODNESS (II PETER 1:3)

JESUS IS IN ME, I AM IN JESUS; SO I AM MADE PERFECT IN HIM (ST. JOHN 17:23)

JESUS IS THE VINE AND I AM ONE OF HIS BRANCHES; IF THE ROOT BE HOLY, SO ARE THE BRANCHES (ROM 11:16/ST. JOHN 15:5)

I AM HOLY IN ALL THAT I DO, JUST AS HE WHO HAS CALLED ME IS HOLY (I PET 1:15)

I AM A PART OF GOD'S CHOSEN GENERATION, A ROYAL PRIESTHOOD, A HOLY NATION, A PECULIAR PEOPLE AND I SHOW FORTH THE PRAISES OF GOD WHO CALLED ME OUT OF DARKNESS INTO HIS MARVELOUS LIGHT (I PET 2:9)

I AM HOLY BECAUSE THE LORD MY GOD IS HOLY (LEV 19:2)

_____

_____

_____

_____

_____

_____

_____

_____

_____

_____

_____

Allison L. Jordan

_____

_____

_____

_____

_____

_____

_____

_____

_____

_____

_____

WHEN YOU ARE STRUGGLING WITH CELIBACY

AND/OR BEING SINGLE

CONFESS...

I WILL RUN FROM FORNICATION BECAUSE IF I FORNICATE, I WILL BE SINNING AGAINST MY OWN BODY (I COR 6:18)

I WILL NOT FOLLOW THE DESIRES OF MY OLD SINFUL NATURE TO INCLUDE SEXUAL IMMORALITY (FORNICATION); FOR THOSE WHO DO WILL NOT INHERIT THE KINGDOM OF GOD (GAL 5:19,21)

I WILL PRESENT MY BODY A LIVING SACRIFICE; HOLY AND ACCEPTABLE UNTO GOD (ROM 12:1)

MY MAKER IS MY HUSBAND/WIFE; THE LORD OF HOSTS IS HIS NAME (ISAIAH 54:5)

I NO LONGER WALK ACCORDING TO THE COURSE OF THIS WORLD (AS IN TIMES PAST), FULFILLING THE DESIRES OF THE FLESH AND MIND. I HAVE BEEN RAISED UP AND AM SEATED IN A HEAVENLY PLACE TOGETHER WITH CHRIST JESUS (EPH 2: 2-3,6)

WHILE I AM SINGLE, I WILL DEVOTE MYSELF TO THE THINGS OF THE LORD; I WILL BE HOLY IN BODY AND SPIRIT (I COR 7:34)

GOD HAS NOT CALLED ME TO UNCLEANNESS; BUT HOLINESS (I THES 4:7)

I CAN LIVE A CELIBATE LIFESTYLE BECAUSE GREATER IS HE THAT IS IN ME THAN HE THAT IS IN THE WORLD (I JOHN 4:4)

I AM DEAD AND MY REAL LIFE IS HIDDEN WITH CHRIST IN GOD. THEREFORE, I WILL HAVE NOTHING TO DO WITH SEXUAL SIN, IMPURITY, LUST AND SHAMEFUL DESIRES, FOR GOD'S TERRIBLE ANGER WILL COME UPON THOSE WHO INDULGE IN THESE THINGS (COL 3:3,5-6)

I WILL LEARN TO BE CONTENT IN MY STATE OF SINGLENESS (PHIL 4:11)

_____

_____

_____

_____

_____

_____

_____

_____

_____

_____

Allison L. Jordan

_____

_____

_____

_____

_____

_____

_____

_____

_____

_____

_____

WHEN YOU HAVE BEEN ABUSED, BETRAYED OR REJECTED BY SOMEONE YOU LOVED (WHO PROFESSED TO LOVE YOU)

CONFESS...

THE LORD IS CLOSE TO THE BROKENHEARTED AND SAVES THOSE WHO ARE CRUSHED IN SPIRIT (PS 34:18 NIV)

JESUS WAS BETRAYED INTO THE HANDS OF MEN BY JUDAS; NO SERVANT IS GREATER THAN HIS LORD (MATT 17:22, ST.JOHN 13:16, ST. JOHN 15:20)

ALTHOUGH MY WEEPING ENDURES FOR A NIGHT; JOY WILL COME IN THE MORNING (PS 30:5)

JESUS WARNED ME THAT I WOULD BE BETRAYED BY PARENTS, BRETHEN, KINSFOLK AND FRIENDS BUT NOT A HAIR OF MY HEAD WILL PERISH AND IF I STAND FIRM, I WILL GAIN LIFE (LUKE 21:16, 18)

I WILL BLESS GOD, THE FATHER OF MY LORD JESUS CHRIST, THE GOD OF ALL COMFORT (II COR 1:3)

I WILL REMEMBER THAT IT IS BETTER TO PUT MY TRUST IN THE LORD THAN TO PUT MY CONFIDENCE IN MAN (PS 118:8)

I WILL TRUST IN THE LORD WITH ALL MY HEART AND LEAN NOT UNTO MY OWN UNDERSTANDING (PROV 3:5)

I WILL NO LONGER BELIEVE EVERY SPIRIT, I WILL TRY THE SPIRITS WHETHER THEY ARE OF GOD (I JOHN 4:1). AFTER ALL, SATAN CAN DISGUISE HIMSELF AS AN ANGEL OF LIGHT AND SO CAN HIS SERVANTS (II COR 11:14-15)

I WILL LOOK TO JESUS, THE AUTHOR AND FINISHER OF MY FAITH, WHO WAS DESPISED AND REJECTED BY MEN, A MAN OF SORROWS AND FAMILIAR WITH SUFFERING (ISAIAH 53:3/HEB 12:2)

I BELIEVE THAT JESUS HEALS THE BROKENHEARTED (LUKE 4:18)

_____

_____

_____

_____

_____

_____

_____

_____

_____

_____

_____

_____

_____

_____

_____

_____

_____

_____

_____

_____

_____

_____

_____

<u>WHEN YOU ARE CONFUSED OR LACK DIRECTION</u>

CONFESS...

I MUST REMEMBER THAT GOD IS NOT THE AUTHOR OF CONFUSION, BUT OF PEACE (I COR 14:33)

I WILL LET THE PEACE OF CHRIST RULE IN MY HEART (COL 3:15)

I WILL KEEP MY MIND STAYED ON JESUS, I WILL TRUST HIM AND HE WILL KEEP ME IN PERFECT PEACE (ISAIAH 26:3)

I HAVE THE PEACE OF GOD WHICH PASSES ALL UNDERSTANDING AND IT SHALL KEEP MY HEART AND MIND (PHIL 4:7)

I WILL BE STILL AND KNOW THAT MY GOD IS GOD (PS 46:10).

I WILL ALLOW THE HOLY SPIRIT TO GUIDE ME INTO ALL TRUTH AND SHOW ME THINGS TO COME (ST.JOHN 16:13)

I WILL NOT ONLY SEEK PEACE; I WILL PURSUE IT (PS 34:14)

SINCE I LACK WISDOM, I WILL ASK IT OF GOD WHO WILL GIVE IT LIBERALLY TO ME (JAMES 1:5)

I OPERATE IN THE KINGDOM OF GOD WHICH IS RIGHTEOUSNESS, PEACE AND JOY IN THE HOLY SPIRIT (ROM 14:17)

I WILL NOT BE CONFUSED BECAUSE A DOUBLE MINDED PERSON IS UNSTABLE IN ALL HIS WAYS (JAMES 1:8)

I WILL ALLOW MY MIND TO BE CONTROLLED BY THE HOLY SPIRIT WHICH IS LIFE AND PEACE (ROM 8:6)

_____

_____

_____

_____

_____

_____

_____

_____

_____

_____

_____

_____

_____

_____

_____

Allison L. Jordan

WHEN YOU ARE STRESSED OUT OR

OVERWHELMED

CONFESS...

MY HEART IS OVERWHELMED BUT I WILL CRY OUT TO GOD AND HE WILL LEAD ME TO THE ROCK THAT IS HIGHER THAN I (PS 61:2)

JESUS SAID THAT BECAUSE I HAVE LABORED AND AM HEAVY LADEN, I COULD COME TO HIM AND HE WOULD GIVE ME REST (MATT 11:28)

I WILL TAKE JESUS' YOKE UPON MYSELF AND LEARN FROM HIM SO THAT I CAN FIND REST FOR MY SOUL (MATT 11:29)

THOUGH I AM TROUBLED ON EVERY SIDE, I AM NOT DISTRESSED; THOUGH I AM PERPLEXED I AM NOT IN DESPAIR (II COR 4:8)

I LIVE IN THE SHELTER OF THE MOST HIGH, I FIND REST IN THE SHADOW OF THE ALMIGHTY, HE IS MY REFUGE AND MY PLACE OF SAFETY (PS 91:1-2)

THIS TOO SHALL PASS BECAUSE GOD IS ABLE TO MAKE ALL GRACE ABOUND TOWARD ME (II COR 9:8)

I WILL NOT BE DISMAYED BECAUSE THE SOVEREIGN LORD HELPS ME (ISAIAH 50:7)

THIS TRIAL MAY SEEM IMPOSSIBLE, BUT WITH GOD ALL THINGS ARE POSSIBLE (MATT 19:26)

I AM OVERWHELMED BUT YOU ALONE OH GOD KNOW THE WAY I SHOULD TURN (PS 142:3)

I WILL BE OVERWHELMED WITH JOY IN THE LORD MY GOD, FOR HE HAS DRESSED ME WITH THE CLOTHING OF SALVATION AND DRAPED ME IN A ROBE OF RIGHTEOUSNESS (ISAIAH 61:10)

_____

_____

_____

_____

_____

_____

_____

_____

_____

_____

_____

_____

_____

Allison L. Jordan

_____

_____

_____

_____

_____

_____

_____

_____

_____

_____

_____

WHEN YOU HAVE TRANSGRESSED GOD'S LAW (SINNED) AND SATAN TRIES TO CONDEMN YOU

CONFESS...

THERE IS THEREFORE NOW NO CONDEMNATION TO THEM WHICH ARE IN CHRIST JESUS; WHO WALK NOT AFTER THE FLESH, BUT AFTER THE SPIRIT (ROM 8:1 KJV)

MY STEPS ARE ORDERED BY THE LORD...THOUGH I HAVE FALLEN, I AM NOT UTTERLY CAST DOWN; FOR THE LORD UPHOLDS ME WITH HIS HAND (PS 37:23-24)

HE WHO BELIEVES IN HIM IS NOT CONDEMNED; BUT HE WHO DOES NOT BELIEVE IS CONDEMNED ALREADY (ST JOHN 3:18)

I WILL HUMBLE MYSELF, PRAY, SEEK GOD'S FACE AND TURN FROM MY WICKED WAYS...THEN I WILL HEAR FROM HEAVEN AND GOD WILL FORGIVE ME AND HEAL ME (II CHRON 7:14)

I CONFESS MY SINS FOR GOD IS FAITHFUL AND JUST TO FORGIVE ME AND PURIFY ME FROM ALL UNRIGHTEOUSNESS (I JOHN 1:9)

LORD, GOD I ACKNOWLEDGE MY TRANSGRESSIONS AND MY SIN IS EVER BEFORE ME; <u>AGAINST YOU AND YOU ONLY</u> HAVE I SINNED AND DONE WHAT IS EVIL IN <u>YOUR</u> SIGHT. HAVE MERCY ON ME, BLOT OUT MY TRANSGRESSIONS AND CLEANSE ME FROM MY SIN (PS 51:1-4)

I REPENT OF MY SIN AND TURN TO GOD, SO THAT HE WILL CLEANSE ME OF MY SIN AND WONDERFUL TIMES OF REFRESHING WILL COME FROM THE PRESENCE OF THE LORD (ACTS 3:19)

BLESSED IS HE WHOSE TRANSGRESSION IS FORGIVEN, WHOSE SIN IS COVERED (PS 32:1)

ALL LIKE SHEEP HAVE GONE ASTRAY AND TURNED TO HIS OWN WAY, BUT THE LORD GOD HAS LAID MY INIQUITY ON JESUS (ISAIAH 53:6)

I CONFESS MY SIN AND RENOUNCE IT SO THAT I MAY FIND MERCY, BECAUSE HE WHO CONCEALS HIS SINS WILL NOT PROSPER (PROV 28:13)

_____

_____

_____

_____

_____

_____

_____

_____

Allison L. Jordan

_____

_____

_____

_____

_____

_____

_____

_____

_____

_____

WHEN YOU DON'T FEEL THE PRESENCE OF GOD

OR DON'T THINK YOU ARE HEARING FROM HIM

CONFESS...

O LORD, I ENTER INTO YOUR GATES WITH THANKSGIVING AND YOUR COURTS WITH PRAISE. I GIVE THANKS TO YOU AND PRAISE YOUR NAME FOR YOU ARE GOOD. YOUR LOVE ENDURES FOREVER AND YOUR FAITHFULNESS CONTINUES THROUGH ALL GENERATIONS. (PS 100:4-5)

LORD, MY LORD, HOW EXCELLENT IS YOUR NAME IN ALL THE EARTH AND YOU HAVE SET YOUR GLORY ABOVE THE HEAVENS (PS 8:1)

MY SOUL BLESSES YOU OH LORD, WITH ALL THAT IS WITHIN ME. I BLESS YOUR HOLY NAME AND I REMEMBER ALL OF YOUR BENEFITS (PS 103:1-2)

AS A DEER PANTS FOR STREAMS OF WATER, MY SOUL LONGS FOR YOU. MY SOUL THIRSTS FOR YOU O GOD, THE LIVING GOD. (PS 42:1)

I LOVE YOU LORD BECAUSE YOU HEARD MY CRY AND MY SUPPLICATION. DEATH HAD ITS HANDS AROUND MY THROAT; THE TERRORS OF THE GRAVE OVERTOOK ME, AND I SAW ONLY TROUBLE AND SORROW BUT YOU TURNED YOUR EAR TO ME AND I WILL CALL ON YOU AS LONG AS I LIVE. (PS 116:1-3)

SEARCH ME, O GOD AND KNOW MY HEART; TEST ME AND KNOW MY ANXIOUS THOUGHTS. SEE IF THERE IS ANY OFFENSIVE WAY IN ME, AND LEAD ME IN THE WAY EVERLASTING (PS 139:23-24 NIV)

I ASCRIBE TO YOU O LORD, THE GLORY DUE YOUR NAME AND I WORSHIP YOU RIGHT NOW IN THE SPLENDOR OF YOUR HOLINESS (PS 29:2) AND IN SPIRIT AND IN TRUTH (ST. JOHN 4:24)

MY SOUL GLORIFIES YOU O LORD AND MY SPIRIT REJOICES IN GOD MY SAVIOR; FOR THE MIGHTY ONE HAS DONE GREAT THINGS FOR ME. HOLY IS YOUR NAME (LUKE 1:46 - 49)

IN YOU O LORD, I LIVE, MOVE AND HAVE MY BEING. WHILE I LIVE I WILL PRAISE YOU LORD; I WILL SING PRAISES TO MY GOD WHILE I HAVE MY BEING (ACTS 17:28, PS 146:2)

YOURS, O LORD IS THE GREATNESS AND THE POWER AND THE GLORY AND THE MAJESTY AND THE SPLENDOR, FOR EVERYTHING IN HEAVEN AND EARTH IS YOURS (I CHRON 29:11 NIV)

_____

_____

_____

_____

Allison L. Jordan

WHEN YOU ARE HAVING TROUBLE WITH

OBEDIENCE

CONFESS...

TEACH ME, O LORD, TO FOLLOW YOUR DECREES; THEN I WILL KEEP THEM TO THE END. GIVE ME UNDERSTANDING, AND I WILL KEEP YOUR LAW AND OBEY IT WITH ALL MY HEART. DIRECT ME IN THE PATH OF YOUR COMMANDS, FOR THERE I FIND DELIGHT. (PS 119:33-35 NIV)

IF I REALLY LOVE JESUS; I WILL OBEY HIS COMMANDS (ST.JOHN 14:15)

I WILL COMMIT MY WAY UNTO THE LORD, KEEP TRUSTING IN HIM AND CONTINUE TO DO GOOD (PS 37:5)

I WILL REMEMBER THAT OBEDIENCE IS BETTER THAN SACRIFICE (I SAM 15:22)

OBEDIENCE TO GOD'S INSTRUCTIONS WILL GIVE ME LIFE (EZE 20:13 NLT)

I WILL BE CAREFUL TO LIVE IN OBEDIENCE TO THE LORD MY GOD SO THAT I MAY BECOME POWERFUL IN HIM (II CHRON 27:6)

I WILL OBSERVE THE COMMANDS OF THE LORD MY GOD, I WILL WALK IN HIS WAYS AND REVERE HIM (DEUT 8:6)

GOD'S LOVE WILL NOT TRULY BE MADE COMPLETE IN ME UNTIL I OBEY HIS WORD (I JOHN 2:5 NLT)

I MUST NOT JUST LISTEN TO THE WORD AND DECEIVE MYSELF; I MUST DO WHAT IT SAYS (JAMES 1:22)

IF I SAY I LIVE IN CHRIST JESUS, I MUST WALK IN OBEDIENCE JUST AS HE DID (I JOHN 2:6)

_____

_____

_____

_____

_____

_____

_____

_____

_____

_____

_____

_____

_____

_____

Allison L. Jordan

_____

_____

_____

_____

_____

_____

_____

_____

_____

_____

<u>WHEN YOU ARE GRIEVING OVER THE DEATH OF</u>

<u>A LOVED ONE</u>

CONFESS...

AS A MOTHER COMFORTS HER CHILD, I WILL RELY ON MY GOD TO COMFORT ME IN THIS TIME OF SADNESS (ISAIAH 66:13)

I MUST ACCEPT THAT THERE IS A TIME TO BE BORN AND A TIME TO DIE; A TIME TO WEEP, A TIME TO MOURN (ECCL 3:2,4)

I THANK GOD THAT BLESSED ARE THEY THAT MOURN, FOR THEY SHALL BE COMFORTED (MATT 5:4)

I WILL BE COMFORTED IN THE KNOWLEDGE THAT ALTHOUGH MY LOVED ONE IS NOW ABSENT FROM THE BODY; THEY ARE PRESENT WITH THE LORD (II COR 5:8)

I WILL SEEK WISDOM, POWER, COUNSEL AND UNDERSTANDING FROM GOD; FOR THEY ARE HIS (JOB 12:13)

IT IS WRITTEN THAT MAN IS LIKE TO VANITY; HIS DAYS ARE LIKE A SHADOW THAT PASSES AWAY (PS 144:4)

WHEN TIMES WERE GOOD, I WAS HAPPY; NOW THAT TIMES ARE BAD I MUST REMEMBER THAT GOD HAS MADE THE ONE AS WELL AS THE OTHER (ECCL 7:14)

I WILL REMEMBER THAT PRECIOUS IN THE SIGHT OF THE LORD IS THE DEATH OF HIS SAINTS (PS 116:15)

IT IS WRITTEN THAT MAN IS JUST A VAPOR THAT APPEARS FOR A LITTLE TIME AND THEN VANISHES AWAY (JAMES 4:14)

IT IS WRITTEN THAT THE RIGHTEOUS PASS AWAY AND THE GODLY OFTEN DIE BEFORE THEIR TIME BECAUSE GOD IS PROTECTING THEM FROM THE EVIL TO COME. THEREFORE I AM COMFORTED THAT MY LOVED ONE IS RESTING IN PEACE (ISAIAH 57:1-2)

_____

_____

_____

_____

_____

_____

_____

_____

_____

_____

_____

_____

Allison L. Jordan

_____

_____

_____

_____

_____

_____

_____

_____

_____

_____

_____

_____

WHEN YOU MUST DEAL WITH DIFFICULT PEOPLE

CONFESS...

Allison L. Jordan

I WILL BE COMPLETELY HUMBLE, GENTLE, AND PATIENT, BEARING WITH OTHERS IN LOVE (EPH 4:2)

I WILL NEVER LET LOVE AND FAITHFULNESS LEAVE ME. I WILL BIND THEM AROUND MY NECK AND WRITE THEM ON THE TABLET OF MY HEART (PROV 3:3)

I WILL OPERATE IN THE FRUIT OF THE SPIRIT WHICH IS LOVE, PEACE, JOY, PATIENCE, KINDNESS, GENTLENESS, FAITHFULNESS, GOODNESS AND SELF CONTROL (GAL 5:22-23)

I WILL BE GRACIOUS AND COMPASSIONATE BECAUSE THE LORD, MY GOD AND FATHER IS GRACIOUS AND COMPASSIONATE (PS 111:4)

I WILL NOT LET EVIL THOUGHTS TOWARD OTHERS PROCEED OUT OF MY HEART FOR AS A MAN THINKETH IN HIS HEART, SO IS HE (PROV 23:7)

I WILL LET THE WORDS OF MY MOUTH AND THE MEDITATIONS OF MY HEART TOWARDS OTHERS BE PLEASING IN MY LORD AND REDEEMERS SIGHT (PS 19:14)

I WILL OBEY JESUS' COMMAND TO LOVE OTHERS AS HE HAS LOVED ME (ST.JOHN 15:12)

I AM ONE OF GOD'S CHOSEN PEOPLE, HOLY AND DEARLY LOVED, THEREFORE, I WILL CLOTHE MYSELF WITH COMPASSION, KINDNESS, HUMILITY, GENTLENESS AND PATIENCE. I WILL MAKE ALLOWANCES FOR THE FAULTS OF OTHERS AND I WILL FORGIVE THEM BECAUSE THE LORD HAS FORGIVEN ME (COL 3:12-13)

I WILL OBEY GOD'S COMMAND TO SHOW MERCY AND COMPASSION TO OTHERS (ZECH 7:9)

IF I SAY I LOVE GOD WHOM I HAVE NOT SEEN, THEN I MUST LOVE MY BROTHER WHOM I CAN SEE ALSO (I JOHN 4:21)

_____

_____

_____

_____

_____

_____

_____

Allison L. Jordan

_____

_____

_____

_____

_____

_____

_____

_____

_____

_____

WHEN YOU ARE HAVING NEGATIVE OR UNGODLY

THOUGHTS

CONFESS...

I WILL CAST DOWN IMAGINATIONS AND EVERY HIGH THING THAT EXALTS ITSELF AGAINST THE KNOWLEDGE OF GOD AND I WILL BRING INTO CAPTIVITY EVERY THOUGHT TO THE OBEDIENCE OF CHRIST. FOR THE WEAPONS OF MY WARFARE ARE NOT CARNAL BUT MIGHTY THROUGH GOD TO THE PULLING DOWN OF STRONGHOLDS (II COR 10:4-5)

I REJECT THAT THOUGHT SATAN, FOR YOU ARE THE FATHER OF ALL LIES AND THERE IS NO TRUTH IN YOU (JOHN 8:44)

I WILL NOT BE CARNALLY MINDED FOR TO BE CARNALLY MINDED IS DEATH; I WILL BE SPIRITUALLY MINDED FOR TO BE SPIRITUALLY MINDED IS LIFE AND PEACE (ROM 8:6)

I WILL THINK ON THINGS THAT ARE TRUE, HONEST, JUST, PURE, LOVELY AND OF GOOD REPORT (PHIL 4:8)

WHEN THOUGHTS FROM THE ENEMY COME IN LIKE A FLOOD, I WILL LET THE SPIRIT OF THE LORD LIFT UP A STANDARD AGAINST THEM (ISAIAH 59:19)

I WILL KEEP MY MIND ON THINGS OF THE SPIRIT RATHER THAN THINGS OF THE FLESH (ROM 8:5)

GET BEHIND ME SATAN! YOU ARE NOT MINDFUL OF THE THINGS OF GOD (MATT 16:23, MARK 8:33)

I WILL KEEP MY THOUGHTS PURE SO THAT I WILL BE BLESSED AND SEE GOD (MATT 5:8)

GOD HAS PUT HIS LAW ON MY MIND AND WRITTEN IT ON MY HEART; HE IS MY GOD AND I AM HIS CHILD (JER 31:33)

I WILL KEEP MY MIND ON THINGS ABOVE AND NOT ON WORLDLY THINGS (COL 3:2)

_____

_____

_____

_____

_____

_____

_____

_____

_____

_____

Allison L. Jordan

WHEN YOU GET ANGRY

CONFESS...

Allison L. Jordan

I WILL NOT SIN BY LETTING ANGER GAIN CONTROL OVER ME, I WILL THINK ABOUT IT OVERNIGHT, SEARCH MY HEART AND BE SILENT (PS 4:4)

I WILL REFRAIN FROM ANGER AND RAGE; IT ONLY LEADS TO EVIL (PS 37:8)

I MUST BE SLOW TO ANGER AND INSTEAD SHOW MERCY, GRACIOUSNESS, LOVE AND TRUTH JUST LIKE THE LORD SHOWS TOWARD ME (PS 86:15, 103:8, 145:8, EX 34:6)

I WILL NOT BE A FOOL AND GIVE IN TO ANGER; I WILL BE WISE AND KEEP IT UNDER CONTROL (PROV 29:11)

I WILL NOT BE QUICK-TEMPERED OR ALLOW MY SPIRIT TO BE PROVOKED FOR ANGER IS THE FRIEND OF FOOLS (ECCL 7:9)

I WILL NOT SUBJECT MYSELF TO GOD'S JUDGMENT BY BEING ANGRY WITH ANYONE (MATT 5:22)

ANGER IS NOT A FRUIT OF THE SPIRIT AND IT WILL KEEP ME FROM INHERITING THE KINGDOM OF GOD (GAL 5:20-21)

I WILL NOT LET THE SUN GO DOWN ON MY ANGER BECAUSE ANGER GIVES A MIGHTY FOOTHOLD TO THE DEVIL (EPH 4:26-27)

I WILL RID MYSELF OF ANGER FOR I HAVE STRIPPED OFF MY OLD EVIL NATURE AND CLOTHED MYSELF WITH A BRAND NEW NATURE THAT IS CONTINUALLY BEING RENEWED IN KNOWLEDGE AFTER THE IMAGE OF JESUS CHRIST WHO PUT THIS NEW NATURE IN ME (COL 3: 8-10)

ANGER CAN NEVER MAKE THINGS RIGHT IN GOD'S SIGHT; THEREFORE I WILL BE QUICK TO LISTEN, SLOW TO SPEAK AND SLOW TO ANGER (JAMES 1:19-20)

_____

_____

_____

_____

_____

_____

_____

_____

_____

Allison L. Jordan

_____

_____

_____

_____

_____

_____

_____

_____

_____

_____

WHEN YOU ARE WAITING FOR YOUR MIRACLE

CONFESS...

THE LORD IS MY PORTION; THEREFORE I WILL WAIT FOR HIM, FOR THE LORD IS GOOD TO THEM WHOSE HOPE IS IN HIM AND TO THE ONE WHO SEEKS HIM (LAM 3:24-25)

OH, THAT YOU WOULD BLESS ME AND ENLARGE MY TERRITORY! LET YOUR HAND BE WITH ME, AND KEEP ME FROM HARM (I CHRON 4:10)

I WILL CALL THOSE THINGS THAT BE NOT AS THOUGH THEY WERE FOR MY GOD IS ABLE TO DELIVER ME (ROM 4:17, DAN 3:17)

I WILL LIFT UP MINE EYES UNTO THE HILLS WHERE MY HELP COMES FROM THE LORD WHO MADE THE HEAVENS AND THE EARTH (PS 121:1-2)

I WILL LOOK TO THE LORD AND CONFIDENT IN HIM WILL I KEEP WATCH; I WILL WAIT WITH HOPE AND EXPECTANCY FOR THE GOD OF MY SALVATION; MY GOD WILL HEAR ME (MICAH 7:7)

I GIVE HONOR AND GLORY TO HIM WHO IS ABLE TO DO IMMEASURABLY MORE THAN ALL I ASK OR IMAGINE, ACCORDING TO THE POWER THAT IS AT WORK WITHIN ME (EPH 3:20-21)

I PRAY THAT YOU WILL BE GRACIOUS, O LORD AND DO A MIGHTY MIRACLE FOR ME AS YOU HAVE DONE IN THE PAST (JER 21:2)

REMEMBER, O LORD, HOW I HAVE WALKED BEFORE YOU FAITHFULLY AND WITH WHOLEHEARTED DEVOTION AND HAVE DONE WHAT IS GOOD IN YOUR EYES (II KINGS 20:2)

LORD, PLEASE DON'T HOLD BACK YOUR TENDER MERCIES FROM ME. MY ONLY HOPE IS IN YOUR UNFAILING LOVE AND FAITHFULNESS (PS 40:11)

LORD, I THANK YOU IN ADVANCE FOR THE MIRACLE YOU WILL PERFORM. IT WILL BRING GREAT HONOR TO YOUR NAME AND IT WILL BE AN EVER-LASTING SIGN OF YOUR POWER AND LOVE (ISAIAH 55:13)

_____

_____

_____

_____

_____

_____

_____

_____

Allison L. Jordan

_____

_____

_____

_____

_____

_____

_____

_____

_____

_____

WHEN YOU ARE HOLDING ON TO UNFORGIVENESS, BITTERNESS OR HATRED CONFESS...

I WILL LET NO BITTER ROOT GROW UP IN ME BECAUSE I DO NOT WANT TO MISS THE GRACE OF GOD (HEB 12:15)

I WILL GET RID OF ALL BITTERNESS, AND I WILL FORGIVE OTHERS SO THAT I DO NOT GRIEVE THE HOLY SPIRIT WITHIN ME. AFTER ALL, GOD THROUGH CHRIST HAS FORGIVEN ME (EPH 4:30-32)

I MUST RID MYSELF OF ALL MALICE, DECEIT, HYPOCRISY, ENVY, AND SLANDER OF EVERY KIND (I PETER 2:1)

IF I SAY I LOVE GOD, YET HATE MY BROTHER/SISTER, I AM A LIAR; FOR IF I CAN'T LOVE MY BROTHER/SISTER THAT I HAVE SEEN, HOW CAN I LOVE GOD WHOM I HAVE NOT SEEN? (I JOHN 4:20)

I WILL FORGIVE THOSE WHO HAVE SINNED AGAINST ME JUST AS I WANT GOD TO FORGIVE MY SINS (LUKE 11:4)

IF MY BROTHER OR SISTER IN CHRIST SINS, I MUST FIRST REBUKE THEM AND IF THEY REPENT, I MUST FORGIVE THEM. (LUKE 17:3-4)

IF I HATE MY BROTHER/SISTER, I AM A MURDERER AND NO MURDERER HAS ETERNAL LIFE ABIDING IN HIM (I JOHN 3:15)

I WILL NOT BE A HATER OF GOD; UNLOVING, UNFORGIVING AND UNMERCIFUL (ROM 1:30-31)

WHEN I PRAY, I MUST FORGIVE EVERYONE I AM HOLDING A GRUDGE AGAINST, SO THAT MY HEAVENLY FATHER WILL FORGIVE MY SINS ALSO (MARK 11:25)

I WILL FORGIVE EVERYONE WHO HAS SINNED AGAINST ME SO THAT MY FATHER WILL FORGIVE ME. IF I DO NOT, MY FATHER WILL NOT FORGIVE MY SINS (MATT 6:14-15)

_____

_____

_____

_____

_____

_____

_____

_____

_____

_____

_____

Allison L. Jordan

_____

_____

_____

_____

_____

_____

_____

_____

_____

_____

<u>WHEN YOU HAVE BEEN DIAGNOSED WITH A</u>

<u>TERMINAL ILLNESS</u>

CONFESS...

MY GOD CAN PERFORM WONDERS THAT CANNOT BE FATHOMED AND MIRACLES THAT CANNOT BE COUNTED (JOB 5:9)

I SHALL NOT DIE BUT LIVE AND DECLARE THE WORKS OF THE LORD (PS 118:17)

THIS SICKNESS WILL NOT END IN DEATH; IT IS FOR THE GLORY OF GOD (JOSH 11:4)

GOD WILL BRING HEALTH AND HEALING; HE WILL HEAL ME AND REVEAL THE ABUNDANCE OF PEACE AND TRUTH (JER 33:6)

THIS BATTLE IS NOT MINE BUT THE LORD'S (I SAM 17:47)

MY HEART HAS KEPT GOD'S COMMANDMENTS; LENGTH OF DAYS, LONG LIFE AND PEACE HAVE BEEN ADDED TO ME (PROV 3:2)

MY FLESH AND MY HEART FAILETH BUT GOD IS THE STRENGTH OF MY HEART AND MY PORTION FOREVER (PS 73:26)

I WILL NOT LOSE HEART FOR ALTHOUGH MY OUTER MAN MAY PERISH, MY INWARD MAN IS BEING RENEWED DAY BY DAY (II COR 4:16)

I WILL CONTINUE TO PROSPER IN ALL THINGS AND BE IN HEALTH JUST AS MY SOUL PROSPERS (III JOHN 1:2)

SURROUND ME WITH YOUR TENDER MERCIES O LORD SO THAT I MAY LIVE, FOR YOUR WORD IS MY DELIGHT (PS 119:77)

_____

_____

_____

_____

_____

_____

_____

_____

_____

_____

_____

_____

_____

_____

_____

_____

Allison L. Jordan

_____

_____

_____

_____

_____

_____

_____

_____

_____

_____

<u>WHEN YOU ARE WEARY OF THE CHRISTIAN WALK</u>

<u>AND FEEL LIKE GIVING UP</u>

CONFESS...

I WILL WAIT UPON THE LORD TO RENEW MY STRENGTH. I WILL MOUNT UP ON WINGS AS EAGLES. I WILL RUN AND NOT BE WEARY, I WILL WALK AND NOT FAINT (ISAIAH 40:31)

I WILL NOT LOSE HEART AND GROW WEARY AND FAINT IN DOING WHAT IS RIGHT, FOR IN DUE TIME AND AT THE APPOINTED SEASON, I SHALL REAP (GAL 6:9)

IN MY WEAKNESS, HIS STRENGTH IS MADE PERFECT AND HIS GRACE IS SUFFICIENT FOR ME (II COR 12:9)

I WILL CONSIDER JESUS WHO ENDURED OPPOSITION FROM SINFUL MEN SO THAT I WILL NOT GROW WEARY AND LOSE HEART (HEB 12:3)

I MUST REMEMBER THAT GOD HAS PROMISED ME THE CROWN OF LIFE IF I PATIENTLY ENDURE TESTING AND CONTINUE TO LOVE HIM (JAMES 1:12)

I WILL LAY ASIDE EVERY WEIGHT AND THE SIN WHICH SO EASILY COMES UPON ME AND CONTINUE TO RUN WITH PATIENCE THE RACE THAT IS SET BEFORE ME (HEB 12:1)

I WILL BE STRONG IN THE LORD AND IN HIS MIGHTY POWER (EPH 6:10)

IT IS GOD WHO WORKS IN ME TO WILL AND ACT ACCORDING TO HIS GOOD PLEASURE (PHIL 2:13)

I WILL BE STRONG AND TAKE HEART, FOR MY HOPE IS IN THE LORD (PS 31:24)

LORD, WHERE CAN I GO TO ESCAPE FROM YOUR SPIRIT? I CAN NEVER GET AWAY FROM YOUR PRESENCE! IF I GO UP TO HEAVEN, YOU ARE THERE AND IF I MAKE MY BED IN HELL, YOU ARE THERE ALSO (PS 139:8)

_____

_____

_____

_____

_____

_____

_____

_____

_____

Allison L. Jordan

ASK JESUS TO SET YOU FREE

Have you ever had so much to do, you didn't know just what to do?
Have you ever felt all alone, the weight of the world was all on you?
Do your footsteps always bring you right back to where you started from?
Did you know that feeling overwhelmed soon leads to being overcome?

Sometimes you feel like giving up, most times you feel like giving in
Out goes all your common sense, sin gradually becomes your friend
A bad person you are not, but you continue to make bad choices
You ignore God's precious spirit; you listen to devilish voices

Satan says; "Come on, sell out to me, just like all the rest...
Before you know what hit you, your life is one big mess?
You feel as if there's just no hope and no one truly cares
Then Satan tells you, "Face it fool, no one really answers prayers"

However, the enemy is a liar, who knows hell is his destiny
He's accepted where he's going so he wants plenty of company
He'll do or say whatever it takes to separate you from Christ
And convince you that after death there could not possibly be life

But there is a man called JESUS, that God rose up from the dead
His life on earth is all you need to dispute what satan said
No matter what you're going through, no matter where you've been
He will bring you out of darkness, he will forgive you of your sins

All you have to do is realize that <u>without God</u>, you are lost
But <u>with God</u> you can start anew; JESUS paid the cost
Don't let satan steal your blessings and rob you of your victory

TAKE OFF THE BLINDERS, GET ON YOUR KNEES, AND

ASK JESUS TO SET YOU FREE!!!

Allison L. Jordan
9/27/96

Allison L. Jordan

ABOUT THE AUTHOR

Allison Lane Jordan is currently pursuing a Masters of Practical Divinity in Biblical Counseling. She has always had a passion for writing both prose and poetry. God has appointed this time for her public debut with *Death And Life Are In The Power Of The Tongue*. Allison resides in Hampton, Virginia with her two children.